Moving Mountains is documents the real-life ex having overcome adversit, have gone on to build meaningful lives, despite the impact of these events having challenged their emotional wellbeing.

The purpose of telling these extraordinary stories is to give hope to others, but more importantly, to understand what lessons we can all learn in terms of how we develop resilience, and what tools we need to deploy to get through the worst that life can present us.

Each book comprises three sections:
1) A personal story outlining a setback in the authors' life.
2) An interview with a psychotherapist in which he or she helps the author to identify what it was that helped them overcome their difficulty.
3) A summary where the therapist sets out those strategies, strengths and resources that we may all be able to use for ourselves when dealing with difficult and challenging events in our own lives.

We aim for each book to be an inspiration to readers as well as offering practical, down-to-earth advice for all who are seeking emotional stability in challenging times.

In this book, Michael O'Brien talks to Stuart Coulden about the extraordinary events in his life that started when he was wrongfully imprisoned for murder at the age of nineteen, had to deal with the death of two children and subsequently went on to become an award-winning author, campaigner and fundraiser.

OVERCOMING
INJUSTICE AND LOSS

Author – Michael O'Brien
Psychotherapist – Stuart Coulden
Edited by – Malcolm Mckay

To Big David 😊
Bøye ri shes
mr Øael obrien
14/3/2024

Published by Moving Mountains.

ISBN (Print): 978-1-911124-80-1
ISBN (Ebook): 978-1-911124-79-5

Michael O'Brien Biography.

Michael O'Brien is the co-founder and chairman, of the Dylan O'Brien Foundation, established after the death of his son Dylan from a metabolic illness. The Foundation aims to raise awareness of genetic metabolic disorders and to supply equipment to improve their quality of life. Michael is also an Award-Winning co-author of *The Death of Justice*, and *Prisons Exposed*. He has been a fervent campaigner for victims of Miscarriages of Justice. Michael is from Cardiff.

Stuart Coulden Biography.

Stuart is a psychotherapist and emotional wellbeing consultant. He has worked with children and adults who are experiencing emotional health difficulties as well as training other professionals in how to offer practical help and support to others. He is a firm believer in demystifying mental health and understanding what it truly means to be human. Stuart is from Norfolk and currently lives in Hertfordshire, UK.

Michaels Story.

On the night of Monday, 12th of October 12,1987 a Cardiff newsagent named Phillip Saunders was battered over the head five times as he arrived home. A short time earlier at about 11.05pm he had been finishing his working day with a drink at his local pub. He then drove home. At 11.19pm an anxious neighbour rang 999 and Mr Saunders was found lying in the small back garden of his home. He died five days later from his injuries.

On the night in question Darren Hall, Ellis Sherwood and I were out trying to steal a car and were pulled in by the police on the 1st of November 1987. After 3 days of questioning Darren Hall confessed to being a look-out whilst Ellis and I murdered Phillip Saunders. He also gave numerous other statements. Even though Darren had confessed to his role in the murder the police did not believe him, and we were released on bail until December. After further inquiries we were again arrested and charged for the murder of Phillip Saunders. We were remanded in custody until the trial.

The evidence against us was; the false confession of Darren Hall (he made 14 different statements to the Police); a statement from a police officer who alleged that Ellis Sherwood and I confessed whilst we were in the police cells and he scribbled down what we were alleged to have said, and statements from 5 witnesses who had long criminal records and had something to gain by saying Ellis and I admitted to them that we had murdered Mr Saunders. There was no forensic evidence to link any of us to the crime.

Whilst on remand my daughter Kylie died of cot death. She was only 3 months old. I was devastated.

Three months later we went to trial on the 27th of June, 1987, and were all found guilty of murder. Not only did I have to deal with my daughter's death I also had to deal with a wrongful conviction. I was just 20 years old and to top it all off my wife walked out on me too.

Whilst serving my sentence my step-dad died, and this took a lot out of me. I could not believe this was all happening. It took me awhile to adjust to prison life and to get the fire in the belly to fight back. However that is what I did by studying law, and I slowly built up a campaign from my prison cell to fight this injustice. I even took the authorities to court over banning journalists from visiting me and made legal history when I was vindicated in the House of Lords in 1999.

After 11 years and 43 days and after the Criminal Cases Review Commission took up our case, we were all released pending a new appeal after fresh evidence had come to light to show we were innocent. A year later we cleared our names.

Since my release, I have attended college and got my A levels in Law, attended Glamorgan University and have tried to turn the negative things which have happened to me into more positive ones. I try and help the youngsters stay away from crime and give lectures wherever possible.

By 2007 I had a nice home, was financially secure, and was determined to rebuild my life. After three years without a relationship, I felt like I had been on my own with my son Kyle way too long and was missing that very important chemistry with a nice lady to make my life complete.

I was sitting in front of the computer one night and decided to do something about it. If I was going to find the right woman she would have to accept Kyle and I as a package. After giving it some thought I decided to go on a site called Dating For Parents which is where I met Claire. Her profile seemed to jump out at me. I was a single dad with one child and she was a single mum with three, who shared similar interests. The age gap between us was 13 years, but we didn't see it as a problem. We started talking in early February 2007 on the internet and phone, getting to know each other as much as we could. We regularly chatted through the night whilst the kids were asleep and I ended up racking up high phone bills on a number of occasions. We were in contact with each other several times a day.

We both decided one night it was time to meet. It just felt right for both of us and we set a date for me to go to Boston in Lincolnshire. I was a gentleman and booked in a hotel near her home. When the day finally arrived to meet I got my train tickets and ended up getting on the wrong train. Claire thought

I was doing a no show. However once I got a signal on my phone I texted her and told her what had happened. I was a hour late. Claire was waiting for me in Boston train station. It was there we shared our first kiss.

We went to a local pub for something to eat and I later walked her back to her home, where I met her three children who should have been in bed but were being nosey to see who was down stairs. One by one they came down and were giggling and pretending to be shy.

Shannon was the oldest at 9 years of Age, Stefan the second eldest was 8 and little Courtney was 6. I spoke to them for a while, but Claire was anxious that they go back to bed because it was getting late and they had school in the morning.

I decided it was time to go back to the hotel to get some sleep and would see them all the next day, when I met them all outside their school. After we'd taken them in Claire and I went shopping and bought some clothes for them. At 3 o'clock that day we picked them up, went straight home and surprised them with their new clothes. Their faces were a picture to see and they were being so excited. I can remember that night going out for tea and then back to Cardiff shortly afterwards. It took nearly 4 hours to get back to Cardiff and I rang Claire to let her know I got home okay.

Things went really well with Claire and we continue to keep in contact via phone, email and face book. I used to speak to Claire every single day. My phone bills were absolutely horrendous, not that I minded, and I did seem to build up a good rapport with the kids too.

I remember our second time together. The trains were not running due to the bad weather so I paid for a taxi for Claire and the kids to come down from Boston to Cardiff to spend some time with each other.

Things were really going well for me with Claire and the kids and I felt maybe that it was time we were a proper family. I asked Claire and the kids to move in with me in Cardiff and all agreed on a new start. I was not impressed with their schools in Boston which clearly lacked funding. Where I was living at the time we had the best schools in Cardiff, Hawthorn Junior School and Whitchurch High, and we had these in mind for when the children moved down. Both these schools would give the children

Michael O'Brien

the opportunities that their old schools couldn't provide.

When the day came we hired a van and a man who loaded up all the furniture from Claire's home. We put the kids in the car and drove to Cardiff. The kids were so excited for a new beginning. We all were. We had some fun with the kids unpacking all the boxes and trying to place all the stuff in the house, but most got stuck in the garage as there was no room for more furniture.

First thing we did was try and arrange a meeting with the schools. We knew if we could get the kids settled the easier it would be for them to adjust to their new home. Our fears were unfounded, and they settled quite quickly into their new schools to our relief.

It was only four months away from Christmas and we wanted to make sure the kids had the best time ever. While the kids were in school Claire and I went shopping for presents. Like most parents we thought we hadn't got enough and worried they weren't going to like what we'd bought, so we ended up doing countless shopping trips right up until the big day. We invited my Mum Marlene down for Christmas and had a good family feast. I ate so much I felt like

Big Bill from Rhyl. Christmas and New Year came so fast and before we knew it we were in 2008.

I had a busy year ahead as I was just about to publish my book *The Death of Justice* which is my autobiography, and although it's inappropriate to go into detail here it was to describe my extraordinary experiences in life before I met Claire and the children. Doing personal appearances, book signings, interviews with the media and TV programmes took up most of my time in 2008. Basically it was just none stop. Before I knew it Christmas was upon us, and there we were running around trying to get presents again for the kids. It was a good time and the highlight for me, as always, was hearing the kids' squeals of delight when they got what they wanted. It made me one happy Dad.

In 2009 Claire and I decided to make our family complete by trying for a baby. In early March our wish came true when Claire got a home pregnancy test and the doctors later confirmed that she was 10 weeks pregnant. I couldn't believe it at first and it took a while before it sunk in. I was going to be a dad again at the age of 42. It was a wonderful feeling and I was on cloud nine for weeks. I had no idea if it was a boy or a girl. We both were thinking up names for both sexes. My best one was Owain Glyn Dwr O'Brien if it was a boy and for a girl she was going to be called Latisha.

I was a bit worried about having another child. My oldest Kyle was 24 and I had lost a child Kylie to cot death previously with my first wife. I can recall mentioning my concerns to the midwife who came to see Claire during her pregnancy. She dismissed my concerns out of hand and thought I was worrying over nothing. This would later come back to haunt her.

Not long after we found out about Claire's pregnancy we were driving towards Cardiff Bay when I asked her would she marry me. She slammed on the breaks in shock and said yes with a beaming smile.

As we set about planning the wedding for December we both realised Claire would be 8 months pregnant and a honeymoon abroad would be out of the question unless we went early. So we booked a holiday in Spain at a lovely place called Tossa De Mar.

The holiday was superb and the weather lovely but the best part was just being with Claire and spending that quality time together. We returned back home after our holiday in a very positive mood.

All we wanted to do was to see the kids. We did miss them. They had stayed with their father whilst we were away and went to pick them up.

The date for the wedding was set for the 5th of December 2009 a month before the baby was due and there was so much to do. We were going to hire a hall and have a big party, however with Claire being eight months pregnant she decided she would rather have the reception at our house.

Soon the big day was upon us. We ordered a limo and arrived in style. There were two funny moments. The first, where I fluffed my lines, and the second when ITV Wales News came racing into the reception with a camera crew and said, 'Sorry we are late!' Everybody saw the funny side and we later found out that during the half time football scores they had announced that we had got married! Now that was amazing!

My life was getting better and better and a few months later our baby was on 4 of February 2010. I could not have been happier. We were both excited to find out it was a boy. After much thought we changed our minds and decided to name him Dylan after the famous Welsh poet Dylan Thomas.

At the birth the consultant paediatrician noted and was concerned about the shape and size of Dylan's head. They felt it was too large and oddly shaped. They also noted a knot in the umbilical cord. Nothing else was observed or noted at the time.

Dylan was allowed home with us the next day and we both noticed that he had slept right through the night and had to be woken up to be fed. We didn't think this was right and raised these concerns to the ward staff at the hospital. They reassured us it was normal, and we were basically brushed off as worrying over nothing.

We took Dylan home and there were early signs something was not right. We didn't think it was *'normal'* for a baby to sleep through the night and most of the day we had to wake Dylan up for his feeds at regular intervals He seemed very lethargic all the time.

When Claire took Dylan to see the consultant for his eight week test, she commented that he was a funny looking kid. It was about this time that Dylan started vomiting a lot and we did not get much sleep due to his vomiting and going blue in the face. We regularly had to tip him over the side of the bed and he was sick and choked at least twice a night. We were both scared at what was happening to him. We had never encountered anything like this before and we were both experienced parents. We were very concerned and brought it to the attention of the doctors who passed it off as a viral infection.

Dylan came down with measles and we were told by the receptionist not to bring him to the surgery and we heeded the advice given. However we were told a few days later that Dylan should have been seen by a Doctor.

Dylan was constantly being ill but despite all this he was a happy child and very rarely cried. The first eight months of his Life consisted of numerous infections and being violently sick on a daily and nightly basis. He failed to put on weight, contracted conjunctivitis and suffered serious development delay.

There were few in a medical professionals that would listen to the concerns my wife and I had. By now we were scared out of our wits, not knowing what was wrong with Dylan and felt very much alone in our fight to establish what these symptoms were so we could get treatment for our son.

Michael O'Brien

Dylan was referred to Community Paediatrics In March 2011. One doctor, after becoming increasingly concerned about Dylan's failure to thrive, pointed out that our son was 15 months old and his weigh was 7.98kg. This was the same weight as he had been in November 2010.

After months of going back and forth to the doctors and hospitals we went to our MP with our concerns. He wrote to the health board and they wrote back apologising for the delays in referring Dylan to a specialist.

Some months later when Dylan Saw one specialist Who was concerned to get Dylan's tonsils out as soon as possible as they were obstructing his airways. The operation was to take place in March 2012, but was cancelled due to lack of beds.

A second Operation was scheduled to take place in April 2012 however Dylan was too ill on that occasion to have the operation and this too had to be cancelled.

It was becoming clear that there was possibly a deeper problem and that genetic testing was needed. So between these cancelled operations we were trying to chase up a referral for genetic testing. We were supported in this by our Health Visitor who was at that time the only professional trying to help us and who saw for herself how ill Dylan was. She came to see us over 50 times and felt, like us, that something was not right with Dylan. But none of us knew what it was.

We were belatedly contacted by the genetics department to do a family history check. However no date for further testing came through which caused further distress to us.

A third operation for the removal of the tonsils was scheduled to take place in May 2012 however Dylan was too ill to have that operation and again this too was cancelled.

An appointment for genetic testing finally came through just after this, but a fourth operation was scheduled to take place before it could be carried out. But once again this operation was cancelled due to lack of beds. When Claire took the phone call from the hospital anger swept across both our faces and we were numb with shock that they could do this to us yet again.

It seems with the exception of our Health Visitor and our MP that no one in the health profession realised just how ill Dylan was and Claire and I told everyone and anyone who would listen that something's was just not right in relation to Dylan. Most of it clearly fell on deaf ears.

We both felt nearly all alone in our battle to find out what was wrong with him which not only put a strain on our marriage it was also having a massive impact on our health. The endless sleepless nights were having a terrible effect on us all.

Despite all this Dylan often had good days and would run around and play with his siblings and in general was a happy child regardless of his problems.

Although I can remember the doctors saying that they did not think he would ever walk, he never let his disabilities stop him and he used to get around by rolling across the floor. You had to see it to believe it. Dylan touched everyone who came to know him and he did actually learn to walk. Claire and I cried when he took his first steps. It was like a miracle had happened.

Dylan kept us up late on the 14th of June. I remember he was playing peek-a-boo and hiding behind the bedroom door. He came up to me and gave me a kiss. I said that's nice Dylan and we had a cuddle on the sofa. It was gone past 12 o clock before we all went to bed.

He did not have a good night's sleep and we were woken up at 2am. He had started choking and Claire tipped him over the side of the bed as he vomited.

This usually happened about two or three times a night but this was different. He wouldn't stop crying so I picked him up and took him into the living room and tried to rock him to sleep. It took me nearly an hour but finally I succeeded at 2.55 am.

Friday the 15th of June 2012 was just like any other weekday with the usual routine of getting the older kids up for school. It was about 8 am that I heard a loud scream from the bedroom. It was Claire. I thought Dylan was having another episode of being violently sick but it became clear that it was worse than that as she came running into the front room with him. He wasn't breathing. We lay him on the floor and we both attempted to resuscitate him. We weren't getting a response so I immediately rung 999 and called for an ambulance. The kids walked in while all this was going on and they let out a scream. I pushed them out of the front room.

Michael O'Brien

I knew things were not looking good and it seemed to take forever for the ambulance and crew to get to us. They tried resuscitating Dylan, then they whisked him in the ambulance, sirens blaring, to the hospital. Claire followed the ambulance in her car, as I did my best to get the kids to school. I then jumped in a taxi and went straight to the hospital.

The hospital staff came to see us and said they couldn't do anything. Dylan was pronounced dead at 8.44.pm. We were totally devastated and could not believe he was gone. The day before he was playing hide and seek with me with no indications that he had a life-threatening illness. The next minute he was dead.

I felt so numb and totally in shock. We all were. At the Inquest months later the pathologist said Dylan died of enlarged tonsils and a metabolic or genetic disease. If only had they listened to us.

An investigation by the health board into Dylan's death indicated that had he had the operation on his tonsils he would still be alive now. They admitted liability for his death.

When we lost Dylan, we were all over the place. But we had another young son, Dainton, to look after, and we had to put a brave face on for him and our older children.

Claire and I had two stark choices facing us. We could launch a media campaign to go after these doctors and try and get them charged with manslaughter or we could do something positive. My gut feeling at the time was to go after the doctors. I wanted them locked up and put in Prison. It took awhile to come to a decision and it took something extraordinary to happen to me before I made my mind up. This is what happened.

My sister Tina and I were with my son, Dainton, in the room where Dylan had passed away. Dainton looked at me and said, 'Daddy, Dylan's here,' and he tried to give Dylan his bottle. Then he talked to his brother for at least 20 minutes. All my sister and I could do was cry. Dainton did not know that Dylan had died in that room, yet we witnessed something I can only describe as very extraordinary and it gave us goose pimples. It was at this moment my faith in God was restored.

I have an IQ of 132 and am not easily fooled. I can assure the reader that what happened that day with Dainton was real and it changed me in lots of ways. I no longer wanted to punish the doctors. I wanted to do something positive which would help others. This is when Claire and I decided to set up an organisation to help children who had suffered in the same way as our son.

The first thing we needed was a name, so after a lot of thought, *The Dylan O'Brien Foundation Voices for Dylan* was born. After considerable help from an agency that helps non-profit organisations, we created a standard constitution setting out our aims and objectives and a few months later we were registered as a not for profit organisation. It was an emotional time for us, but at least now we could start helping others.

The first Child we helped was a five year old boy who was local to us. We read about his story in the daily newspaper. The boy suffered from a rare degenerative condition called Sanfillippo 111, which meant that he was almost totally unable to talk and was only expected to live into his teens. Someone had burgled his home and stolen his Kindle which he'd received as a Christmas present. The boy couldn't read but his father used to play story books on the Kindle which helped him to go to sleep. We were so moved by this that we contacted the newspaper to offer our assistance, and offered to pay for a new Kindle.

I would have liked to have kept this out of the media but there was no way we could and through the newspaper we met the little boy with his father and did a piece for publication. The father said to me, I wake up every day wondering if this is going to be my last day with my boy. It's like a living bereavement not knowing when my boy is going to be taken away from me. We both shared a few tears and hugged each other. The boy's father was aware that one day he would wake up and the inevitable was going to happen. There is no cure for this disease.

Things were still so raw for Claire and me and on the way home from this meeting that we never said a word. It had hit home to us that If Dylan had lived he would have had the same or similar problems as this little boy who although being in a wheelchair most of the time, had made a huge impression on us with his smiles and cheerfulness. He was just an amazing child. It was a great feeling to help him and his father, knowing that Dylan's legacy would live on through the foundation. Seeing that little boys face light up was very humbling.

We found out through the media about another little boy with Scoliosis, a spinal condition which would require a lot of money to put right. His family were raising funds from a car boot sale and the money was stolen from their car. This case touched our heart too. I can recall reading the article and felt we had to do something. We went to visit the grandparents to find out how we could help and wrote a cheque to replace the money which was stolen. A local businessman stepped in and made a donation as did other kind readers of the paper that had reported the story.

We were limited in how we could help financially, but we offered our support to the family and let them know we were there for them. The little boy's family were well organised and raised enough money, so he could have a special back brace fitted to straighten out the spine.

He now is being treated at Great Ormond Street Hospital in London and from the pictures we've seen, the brace appears to be working. As I write this he's due to have further treatment although there are doubts whether the NHS is going to continue to pay for this. This is a worry the family could do without.

The Dylan O'Brien Foundation continue to monitor the progress of this little boy and will help the family as and where needed.

On Facebook we came across the case of a little a little girl who had this disease called West Syndrome. The family were raising funds for her care and we stepped in to see what we could do to help. The girl was so cute it melted your heart. We realised after a short period of time that she and her family couldn't go very far due to the size of their car, as it was too small to take both her and the equipment needed to feed her.

At the time we had a 7-seater car and saw they needed it much more than we did and we ended up donating it to them. To see the look on the family's face was brilliant. We helped to raise funds at different events with them and are alway here when and if they need us.

The foundation has given me a new purpose and saving children's lives is our priority. We supply the hospitals in England and Wales with live saving sleep monitors and supply saturation monitors to check a child's oxygen levels.

We also supply members of the public who have a child with a genetic and or metabolic disorder with lifesaving monitors.

One thing Dylan taught me is that whatever life throws at you; you have to turn all negative situations into positive ones. We all get dealt bad cards from time to time however it how you play those cards that counts.

Dylan's legacy is living on through the foundation and his death has not been in vain. I may have gone through the mill by losing two beautiful children and suffering a miscarriage of justice. However I am a better person for it and have bounced back from these negative things and turned them into positives. I am not a victim at the mercy of events, I am a survivor who is now in a position to help other people. I hope my story will inspire others to do the same.

Interview between Michael and Stuart Coulden, psychotherapist..

1. *The overwhelming theme that springs from anyone who has overcome adversity in their lives is that word 'resilience' - the capacity humans have to recover from difficulties; or mental toughness.*

What do you put your resilience down to? Is it something you feel you inherited or did earlier life experience help you with this strength and determination?

Answer: I put my resilience down to be inherited from my mother who had a tough life but showed great resilience in always having the knack of bouncing back from whatever life threw at her and I seem to have the same traits as her. Some earlier life experiences when I was growing up on a tough council estate also stood me in good stead. Seeing poverty and domestic violence as we were growing up made me determined not to live my life this way and I wanted to better myself. I was also determined that I would not bring up my children in a violent atmosphere like we had then and have kept that promise. It was important for me to break the cycle.

2. *It's interesting that you say that you grew up in a difficult environment. One key person – in this case your mum – was able to show you a different way of doing things, or seeing that life could be different. Looking back to growing up, what strengths did your mum show you specifically? Was there a particular thing you witnessed your mum doing that led to that awareness of difficult situations can be overcome?*

Answer: My mother showed me that even when something bad happens there's always light at the end of the tunnel. She overcame her mother dying at an early age and losing a sister, and showed me that after I lost my own daughter that I could overcome and learn to live with her death too. My mother lost two children too and had a mental strength that you see in very few people. It certainly rubbed off on me and helped me to overcome what life threw at me too. I got my mental strength from my mother that I have no doubt was an amazing woman.

3. *So, by observing how your mother moved forward from such tragic loss in her own life, you were able to bring this to mind when you had to deal with the loss of your own daughter. We often learn how deal with situations by watching those around us. Your mother certainly seems to have been the foundation from which you developed your resilience for dealing with events in your adult life.*

Moving forward to when you were nineteen and had just been found guilty of a serious crime that you hadn't committed, what was going through your mind when left with your own thoughts on that first night in prison?

Answer: When I was found guilty I had lost all hope in the criminal justice system, I was in total despair and felt that God had abandoned me. I thought I was never going to be a free man again and be with my family. I was close to a nervous breakdown. I had suicidal thoughts and wanted to die. At this stage I had no fight in me.

4. *It must have been a desperately low moment in your life. How soon after that night were you able to see a way to giving your life purpose and hope? What did it take for you to change your mindset to one that would move you from feeling suicidal?*

Answer: I first turned to drugs to cope with what happened and it took me two years to get my head together. The turning point for me was meeting other prisoners who were fighting to prove their innocence who helped me get off the drugs, and then I got angry and decided to study law. Then I started fighting back and began educating myself. I dug deep and the strength I got was finding out how this happened to me and how I was going to put it right

5. *Can you remember what any prisoner said to you that gave you the strength to stop the drugs and take more control of your life?*

Answer: One of the prisoners said to me you have got to start writing to people and get focused on fighting to clear your name. No one is going to do it for you. He gave me a rollicking and didn't mince his words. That night as I lay in my bed it sunk in that he was right. So I went to see the psychologists who helped me come off the drugs and started getting counselling. From then on I never looked back and started studying my case and the law and the fight back began.

6. *I think it's true that we can all need someone to break us out of that trance of helplessness and help us look again at our situation. It seems to me that he pointed out a universal truth – we all need to feel we have control over aspects of our life. Even in prison where so much of our lives are controlled by others, we can still take control of key parts.*

Did you then feel you had some purpose or goal in life from that point?

Answer: The more I studied the more determined I became. I didn't have much time for negative thoughts due to the volume of work which needed to be done. I was determined a positive outcome would be established. I knew I was innocent and I was going to prove it. My anger at the injustice done to me drove me on.

7. *Having that drive to achieve a very clear objective - clearing your name - really gave you the focus to channel your emotions into a positive form. This must have been challenged to the extreme when you received the tragic news that your daughter had died. How did you find the strength to cope?*

Answer: When my daughter died I did wonder to myself how much more could I take. However I managed to keep my head together as I had my little boy, Kyle, to think of too. I had a lot to fight for so I could be with my son. I had to deal with the breakup of my marriage. After my daughter died it was just too much for my wife who left me shortly after Kylie passed away. I was determined to remain strong and was going to fight this injustice. My anger was now at boiling point I was not going to take what had happened to me lying down and my desire to overturn this injustice and overcome everything I had been through was so strong.

8. *It's very interesting that you mention the anger. Anger is a very good emotion, if it is deployed in the right amount, at the right time and towards the right place or person. It is clear* *from what you have described that this was exactly what was happening in your case. I am sure that you met people who were as angry as you but who unfortunately, were directing it in the wrong amount and in the wrong place. Did you have anyone to help and guide you during this time?*

Answer: There were a few people who were also fighting to clear their names who gave me the strength and guided me as best they could and we used to stick together a lot and help each other where we could.

9. *Your period of imprisonment was eleven years. Could you give an idea of your daily routine? Did you have a way of making each day count or did you rely on routine?*

Answer: I used routine. I would get up in the morning at unlock, have breakfast, go to work, then work on my case when I got back. I would go to the gym for an hour and after I came back spend the rest of the evening working on my case and studying law into the early hours of the morning. I found going to the gym helped keep my anger under control.

10. *Many clients I've worked with say that putting a routine into their day is a very helpful tool for when they are highly stressed or depressed. Also, when we are highly stressed our brain thinks that we are in physical danger and dumps large amounts of adrenaline and cortisol into our bodies to get us ready to stand and fight or run away. Physical exercise burns these hormones off and replaces them with serotonin and endorphins, both of which lift our mood and enable us to think more clearly. You were clearly deploying excellent stress management techniques Michael. So, talk me through the process of your appeal and subsequent release from prison. I imagine it was an emotional rollercoaster?*

Answer: Our hopes were raised for an appeal after a TV company made a documentary about our case uncovering new evidence in the process. Our case was taken up by the Criminal Cases Review Commission who look at these kinds of cases. They investigated further and found more new evidence. Our case was then referred to appeal. We applied for bail pending the appeal and three days before Christmas in 1999 we were released on bail. I remember coming out of the prison and being surrounded by journalists. My family spotted me and came over and gave me a hug. This was an emotional day for me and my family as we had fought so hard to see this day come and we'd made it happen. I had to wait a year for the appeal to come about. I used that time to help other innocent people and gave talks all over the UK. I also launched a public inquiry campaign into the way the Police and the CPS had handled my case and other cases in Wales. I felt I had to keep busy. When the Appeal came it took the judges 3 minutes to quash the conviction after hearing all the new evidence over a ten-day period. It was an amazing feeling to know I was not regarded as a murderer anymore and the public knew the truth. I was still quite angry at this point because I asked the judges for an apology for what we went through and they ignored me. So I did give them a piece of my mind and was taken out of the court by my barrister. I never did get that apology.

11. *I would say you were quite right to feel anger at not receiving an apology! Sometimes, if we have worked tirelessly to achieve a life goal, when we have achieved it, we can feel rather empty and directionless. It is good to know that you found a new goal to keep you focussed and positive. Helping others can also have a very positive impact on how we feel about ourselves too. So, this major chapter of* *your life was over and you now had to build a new life for yourself. What first steps did you take to adjust to this new life?*

Answer: I started studying law and managed to get my A level in it. I also attended University. I helped set up an organisation to assist the innocent and then started writing my books. I did find it difficult keeping off the drugs due to the depression, however I managed again to overcome this using the same strategy as I used in prison and gained a positive mental attitude. I also spent time with my family and young son and tried to get to know them better.

12. *It must have been a tough time for you. Re-adapting to a different life and environment is really challenging as we must find new ways of getting our emotional needs met. This can take time. You certainly deployed that resilient core you inherited from your mum. By this time, you had started to rebuild your life, but did you think about what may still be missing from your life at that time?*

Answer: I think it hit home that I had lost 11 years of my life when went into a pub and saw 20-year olds enjoying themselves. It hit me how much I had missed out on. I left the pub shortly afterwards because I could not deal with it

13. *I can only imagine how that felt at the time. How long did it take for things like going to the pub and other run of the mill activities like that began to feel normal again? Or have they ever since felt normal?*

Answer: *It took me a few years to adjust to do doing everyday things like going to the pub, being in large crowds or going into town to do shopping.*

14. *You then went on to meet your new partner. When did you begin to feel ready to start a new relationship? Was it a gradual realisation or did you suddenly feel you were ready?*

Answer: I moved into my new home in 2004 and spent three years on my own before feeling it was time for me to find someone to share my life. I realised I was ready for a relationship I had a nice house and money, but I felt it was nothing without a good woman to share it with. I went onto the dating for parents website and this is where I met Claire. It was in 2007 and she had three children and my son was living with me at the time and we hit it off. We spent many hours on the phone and we used to see each other every week even though she lived 220 miles away in Boston, England. It was in 2008 we took the step of moving in together and a year later we married. Claire then gave me the good news that I was going to be a dad again.

15. *Wow, that must have been a really positive step forward for you. Were there any experiences from your previous life that you found got in the way of making the relationship with Claire work from the outset? Some people I have worked with have cited patterns from previous experiences getting in the way of new relationships initially, particularly things like trust, planning for the future etc.*

Answer: It was a really positive step in the right direction and It was difficult to trust at first but I overcame them by being positive and thinking positive.

16. *Are you able to expand on any of those initial difficulties?*

Answer: The initial difficulties I had was one of trust I had a few previous relationships where my compensation was a big issue and I didn't know if they wanted me for me or my money. It soon came out they were after my money so there's where I had problems with the trust issues

17. *I can see that this would have been an issue. How about the need for privacy? This is a basic human need and I'm sure it was difficult to get this when you were in prison. Do you feel you may have initially over-compensated as you adjusted to life on the outside?*

Answer: I couldn't complain about my privacy as I was leading a high-profile campaign when I was released. I don't think I overcompensated as I adjusted to life outside.

18. *So, would you say that at that time in your life, things were going pretty well? A new partner, a family and another child on the way. And then your son Dylan was born. Were you aware he had serious medical issues early on?*

Answer: I felt my life was complete however it became apparent early in Dylan's life that something was wrong with him

19. *Was it you and your wife that first noticed, or was it the medics?*

Answer: It was us. However my sister Tina spotted it could be a genetic disorder and we all started to research it and saw it was more likely than not a genetic or metabolic disease. No one in the medical profession apart from our GP recognised something was wrong

20. *It must have been very frustrating if you were feeling that you weren't being heard. How did you cope with that?*

Answer: I was so frustrated that we weren't being listened to that I ended up going to my MP and asking for help and he wrote a strong letter to the health board on our behalf raising our concerns

21. *And that made the difference? Were Dylan's health issues taken seriously after that?*

Answer: If it wasn't for our MP nothing would have been done. After he stepped in referrals were made to many specialists, however due to the length of time it took to see Dylan and the four cancelled operations in his tonsils, Dylan never did get to see the genetics team before he died.

22. *Another huge tragedy befell you, and yet you have clearly, on many levels, bounced back again. It would be very easy, in that situation, to search around for someone to blame. One of the strengths that has really struck me whilst talking to you is your determination not to be a victim of your circumstances. Instead you find meaning in your situation and use that to focus on the future. Can you tell me more about how you coped in the immediate aftermath of Dylan's death?*

Answer: I did go in on myself when Dylan died and thought I could not take it anymore, however I managed to find the strength after a few months to do something positive and this is where my wife and I decided to set up The Dylan O'Brien Foundation. This would be Dylan's Legacy and his name would live on through the Foundation. We both shared many tears but we felt this was the way forward. We now supply parents and the Hospitals with lifesaving equipment. If Dylan would have had a sleep apnoea alarm he may well be still with us. It has been some comfort to know that the work we are doing with the Foundation is saving children's lives.

23. *Grief is a perfectly normal emotional response and a rule of thumb tends to be that if, after 6 months, we are finding it difficult to reconnect fully with our lives, then it may be helpful to see a therapist or counsellor. Did you and your wife seek out some counselling?*

Answer: We did get counselling and it helped us come to terms with what happened to Dylan and we have managed to rebuild our lives. However it did take a few years to properly come to terms with his death and we have been able to work through it with the work we are doing with the foundation.

24. *The loss of someone close will stay with us for the rest of our lives. It is how we contextualise this loss and integrate the experience into our futures that is the mark of recovery. The energy you and your wife put into establishing Dylan's Foundation – having a focus on a positive force for change can put us back on an emotionally healthy footing. What are the pitfalls in your life now that you need to be wary of in order that you maintain your emotional wellbeing?*

Answer: I find I need to keep away from negative people and focus on what I can do rather than what I cannot do and take each day as it comes.

25. *I think that what you observe here is a very valid point. We can, if we're not careful, find ourselves surrounded by people that can reflect a negative view of our situation – often these people can think that they are being helpful to us. During this discussion I have been struck by your resilience and that innate ability you have had to focus on goals and* *look for the positive in any situation, however awful that situation might be. In conclusion Michael, if you had a friend who was experiencing similar hardships as those that you have been through, what advice would you give them?*

Answer: My advice to anyone who was going through what I experienced is to educate yourself and focus on the task facing you one day at a time. Use your time wisely and surround yourself with positive people who can and will inspire you. Its very important that whatever life throws at you that you are able to take the positives out of the negatives in order to turn your life around like I have. It is not an easy task. However if you want to survive and get through whatever trauma you're experiencing this is the only way forward. You can rebuild your life after a traumatic event and I hope my experiences will help as many people as possible and to inspire them to turn their negative experiences and gain some positive things from it. I do not see myself as a victim I see myself as a survivor with a positive message. One day I hope those suffering or have suffered a traumatic event will do the same.

26. *Thank you so much for agreeing to discuss your life experiences, Michael. One of the pleasures of my job is listening to other people's stories and finding myself humbled at the inner resilience of humans. I am sure there are many useful tips and strategies that you have put forward which can help others who read your account of overcoming such personal hardship.*

Stuart Coulden, Conclusion.

Michaels' story is quite extraordinary. I am sure that many of us could hardly imagine how, in his shoes, we might be able to survive not one, but three incredibly distressing episodes such as his. How do we humans manage to survive difficult situations, challenges that, at the time, feel impossible to overcome?

Navigating the difficulties that can present themselves in any of our lives can be a challenge to our emotional wellbeing, but by tapping into the essence of what it really *means* to be human, and understanding the resources that we have and can deploy when necessary, we find we can be incredibly resilient and able to survive even the toughest of situations. Just as Michael has outlined in his tale.

So, what can we learn from him? How can we give ourselves the best chance of navigating the obstacles that can feel overwhelming to us? And how do we know when we are out the other side?

Let's first look at how our brain reacts to stressful situations.

Stress is something we are all familiar with, it's written about, discussed with friends and colleagues and the word is used to describe a variety of situations that can result in us feeling uncomfortable, anxious, angry, out of control, frozen with fear and in some cases, feeling like a startled rabbit caught in the headlights of an onrushing car and unable to think clearly or act rationally.

Why is that?

Well the answer seems to lie with the most powerful tool human beings possess, and that is our imagination. Much stress and anxiety in our lives comes from overthinking or worrying.

Let's just dissect this a little.

Michael O'Brien

Thousands of years ago worrying ensured our survival. Humans were the feeblest, slowest, most poorly protected food around. 'Man, the hunter' is a hopelessly inaccurate idea, as for most of our evolution we survived by spotting dangerous situations and staying well away. And how did we do that? By worrying. Or put another way; using our thinking ability to explore every possibility before putting ourselves at risk. Possibilities like "There could be a tiger in there", had to be checked out first.

These days few situations threaten our physical survival, but we still behave as if there are many. Most of us face many potentially worry provoking situations every day and if we avoided them all, we'd get nowhere fast, paralysed by panic and indecision.

Our brains still, in this modern age, mistake worry for physical danger and therefore we can experience the extreme emotions associated with fear if we are climbing inside our own head and imagining dreadful outcomes to situations.

Our brain is preparing us to escape a physically dangerous situation by either running away or punching the living daylights out of it. This is known as the *'fight or flight'* mechanism which floods our bodies with chemicals such as adrenaline and cortisol to get our body ready for physical action, we notice this as our heart rate goes up, we hyperventilate, and stomach turns cartwheels as the blood moves rapidly away from our stomach wall, our mouth can become dry and we get very edgy and shaky.

As well as the physical changes to our body, this mechanism changes the way we can think too. When this flight/flight mechanism kicks in we are locked out of our thinking brain. By this I mean the part of our brain that can think through problems, work out creative solutions and see the bigger picture – the shades of grey in a situation if you like. And of course, if we are literally under attack we wouldn't want to spend time thinking, we would want to be acting. However, if the fight/flight mechanism kicks in because of thinking about stuff or playing through worst-case scenarios in our head it can literally make us stupid!

By stupid, I mean we can't access our thinking brain at all and we function out of a very small part of our brain that only does yes/no, always/never, 'black and white' thinking. A clue to this is observing someone who is getting panicky, or angry – their language can appear very 'black and white' – "You *always* do that", "I'll *never* get this right", "The *whole*

Michael O'Brien

world is against me". This why we can all say or do incredibly stupid things when we are under stress – our thinking brain isn't in gear and we can't see the wood for the trees!

I'm sure that Michael found himself in situations where events were so overwhelming that that he couldn't deploy his thinking brain for a while. This is pretty normal, obviously, but the key to unlocking Michaels' subsequent actions was that after the initial shock, he was able to find a way to feel calm enough to take a step back from his situation and begin taking control of it.

So here are some practical tips that we can all use to take control of unhelpful worries.

Take time to think over all your worries, dilemmas and problems. Set aside half an hour for worrying during the day. When you find yourself worrying at any other time, note the worry down and keep it for later. Once you write down your worries, you can be more objective, and 'leave them alone' for a while.

Try using the following template:
1. *"I am worried about..."*
2. *"The worst that could happen is..."*

3. *"The best that could happen is..."*
4. *"Things I can do now are..."*
5. *"Other factors to remember".*

Also realise that tiredness, hunger, anxiety and other 'low' mood states can lead to your thoughts becoming more doom-laden. So, worry after you've eaten, in the morning after a good sleep, or best of all, after 20 minutes exercise

This strategy helps us mentally *take control* of our worries because chronic worrying can quickly make you feel helpless, as you imagine more and more problems until you reach the point where you can't possibly solve them all. It usually goes a bit like "If that happens, then this will happen, and then that will be a disaster!" Instead, try challenging worry-provoking thoughts with questions like "What evidence is there for that?" and "Just how likely is that, based on my past experience?" Learn to distinguish between possibility and probability. It's your mind – *take control* of your thoughts! This whole process can be referred to as **resilience** - the capacity to recover quickly from difficulties, mental toughness.

So, once we've got control of all those worries and our brain is calm enough for us to think clearly, what's the next step we can learn from Michael?

Well Michael always puts together a plan of action – whether it was how he would go about clearing his name after being falsely found guilty of murder, or how he was going to find something meaningful from his son Dylan's' tragic death.

Goal setting is essential – small manageable goals if the overall situation looks too daunting – small steps that take you in the direction you want to travel. This is essential for two reasons:

1. It provides a focus for planning our way out of the situation
2. It gives a clear way to measure our progress

In addition to this, an essential human need is to be *stretched* - to push ourselves through the pain barrier whether that's physical or emotional. Goal setting gives us the opportunity to test ourselves. When we've achieved a goal, it can be interesting to feel the buzz we get from success – it gives us the jolt we need to push ourselves to the next goal.

An interesting side effect of these strategies is that we can find ourselves having a more optimistic outlook on life – even in the direst of situations – and this gives us a more '*can-do*' attitude – resilience!

An example that I give to sixth form students when I speak to them about managing stress is this: imagine that you've just been dumped by the first absolute love of your life. You're devastated, you can't bear to go out, so you put the TV on to take your mind off your unhappiness. But every channel seems to have happy couples, holding hands or kissing. So, you grab your coat and head out to take your mind off your loss, but everywhere you look there are happy couples.

Why is it, when something like this happens, all you see are reminders of your own pathetic situation? It's because our brain just homes in on things that are important to us at that time.

Michael was able to focus on an optimistic outcome because that's what he needed to believe in order to get through those tough challenges. The lovelorn teenager however, was just seeing those things that validated his sense of desperation!

A positive way of seeing things can really help change what we see and feel around us and therefore is highly likely to help us find a creative path through any difficulty.

So, *resilience*, getting our worries under control, seeing the reality of the situation, and setting ourselves practical, achievable goals are the three key pillars to Michael's success. Despite the enormity of his situation, the seemingly insurmountable challenges, the setbacks, losses, and seemingly impossible mountains to negotiate, he has come out the other side with meaning and purpose in his life once more after taking control of his situation.

Finally, I'd like to leave you with a story:

Those of you that have taken a hike in the hills will know just how quickly weather conditions can change – one-minute sun, the next rain, then wind, low cloud, sleet, snow – in fact we can often experience four seasons in one day. It was on a day like this that four friends set off to enjoy a day in the hills, scaling a peak or two and being home in time for a pint in the pub.

As they set out in the morning from their campsite in the valley, the sun was shining, and they could clearly see the path to the top of the first hill, winding its way precariously up the ridge. They set off with spirits high, looking forward to the challenge ahead and the great views they hoped to experience form the top of the hill.

The ascent began gently, but soon the grassland started to give way to the rockier uplands, but still the path drove them upward. Then, almost in an instant, the weather changed. Mist and low cloud tumbled down the hillside to meet them and soon the group were engulfed in a dense, heavy fog.

The group closed in together, the path was becoming more difficult to follow, it was difficult to see their hands in front of their faces. Worried about inadvertently walking off the side of the mountain, the group decided to rope themselves together, nominating the friend in front to slowly inch along the path. The question of course was whether to continue upwards or to try and retrace steps back down and into the valley. It was decided to continue upward.

Michael O'Brien

Fear and trepidation passed through the minds of all four friends as slowly they inched their way forwards, wondering if the next step could be the one that would send them plunging down the steep side of the hill. Slowly, metre by metre they headed blindly up the path, for what seemed like hours, their limbs trembling, adrenaline pumping, unable to trust their senses, until slowly, almost imperceptibly, visibility started to return. The mist started to clear, and the path reappeared.

It was then that the group saw that they were just a short stride from the summit and with new found exuberance the group of friends clambered to the top and congratulated each other for holding their nerve and making it safely.

And it was then that, with a mixture of residual fear, and the exhilaration of their achievement, the group looked down the mountain and could, only now, clearly see the path that they'd so tentatively navigated.

Printed in Great Britain
by Amazon